I'm Going Home. ...Finally!

A Handbook of Everything You Need to Know About Your Newly Adopted Puppy or Dog!

Candace T. Botha

Suncoast Ink publications
Sarasota, FL

Copyright ©2017 Candace T. Botha

All rights reserved. No part of this book may be reproduced or transmitted in any form or by any means, including but not limited to information storage and retrieval systems, electronic, mechanical, photocopy, recording, etc., without written permission from the copyright holder.

Cover Image: Background: Photo©pixabay.com/ZIPNON
Image of dog: Photo©123rf.com/Susan Richey-Schmitz

ISBN: 978-1-64008-060-7

First Printing

Dedication

For the past 10 years, I have had the honor of serving as the publisher of Suncoast Pet, a regional magazine for animal lovers in Southwest Florida that I founded in 2007.

Suncoast Pet has long been an active supporter of area animal groups. The magazine has been committed to helping rescue efforts on Florida's Suncoast by promoting fund-raisers, by spotlighting different animal groups in our community and by including a "Rescue Me" advertising section that includes adoptable dogs and cats in each issue of the magazine, with 50 percent of the proceeds from the cost of the "Rescue Me" ads donated to the shelters and groups that are caring for these animals until their forever homes are found.

During the past decade, I have had the privilege of meeting many men and women—nearly all volunteers—who work tirelessly in animal rescue, saving lives each and every day. Most work full-time jobs to support their families, yet they still spend countless hours after work, on their days off or on weekends at shelters or with animal groups to help socialize, train and find homes for abandoned, ill, injured and homeless animals in our community.

This book is dedicated to these individuals, who often go unnoticed and unrecognized for the compassionate work they do, but who truly are modern-day unsung heroes...not just in my hometown, but also in the global animal community.

It is my hope that people working in animal rescue will discover that this handbook can serve as an extremely valuable tool in sharing information about the animals they have nurtured and loved with their newly adopted families, so that the transition from shelters or foster care to forever homes is as seamless as possible for both dogs and humans.

I encourage animal groups in every part of the country to contact me directly if they are interested in purchasing multiple copies of these handbooks to resell to their volunteers and foster parents. People working in the animal community can purchase copies at a discounted rate and then sell the handbooks for a profit to raise much-needed funds.

If you are interested in purchasing multiple copies for your animal group or shelter, please send an e-mail to suncoastinkpublications@gmail.com.

In closing, let me say that I am humbled by the dedication and commitment I have seen in the animal community in Southwest Florida, and I truly hope this handbook will make the invaluable work of all volunteers and foster families easier.

About the Author

Candace T. Botha has served as the publisher, associate publisher, editor and editorial director of numerous regional publications, including Montage magazine, ITCA Today, Morris County Golfer, Pathways, Sussex County Magazine and Northern Horizons, all published in the state of New Jersey, as well as The VOICE of the Downtown Merchants, published in Sarasota, Florida.

She also is the founder and publisher of Suncoast Pet magazine, an award-winning regional publication for pet owners in Southwest Florida.

In addition to this journal, Botha also is the publisher of "The Ultimate Assignment Journal for Freelance Writers," "The Ultimate Assignment Journal for Freelance Photographers" and "The Ultimate Editorial Planning Journal for Publishers & Editors," as well as "How Blessed Am I—A Weekly Journal for Giving Thanks for Life's Extraordinary Moments."

Especially for animal lovers, she has created "Forever in My Heart—A Journal for Families Who Lovingly Foster Cats & Kittens" and "Forever in My Heart—A Journal for Foster Pup Families." And to complement this title, "I'm Going Home...Finally!— A Handbook of Everything You Need to Know About Your Newly Adopted Kitten or Cat" also is available.

All journals are available on www.amazon.com, www.barnesandnoble.com and other online book retailers.

How to Use This Journal

"I'm Going Home...Finally!" has been especially created for the compassionate men, women and children working in animal rescue.

Simple in format and easy to use, this handbook has been designed to include all of the important information new pet parents can use to best care for the puppies or dogs they bring in to their families.

Foster parents and rescue volunteers are encouraged to record the critical information all new pet owners want—and need—to know about the four-legged friends they adopt or rescue, including:

- A Pup's "Back Story"
- Vaccination History
- Dental Records
- Special Medical Needs
- Favorite Foods
- Favorite Toys & Games
- Sleeping Habits
- Training Experience
- Recognized Commands
- And Much More!

So, grab a pen or pencil and see just how easy it is to create a dog's life story...here in these pages!

Photo©123rf.com/mdorottya

My Life Before You

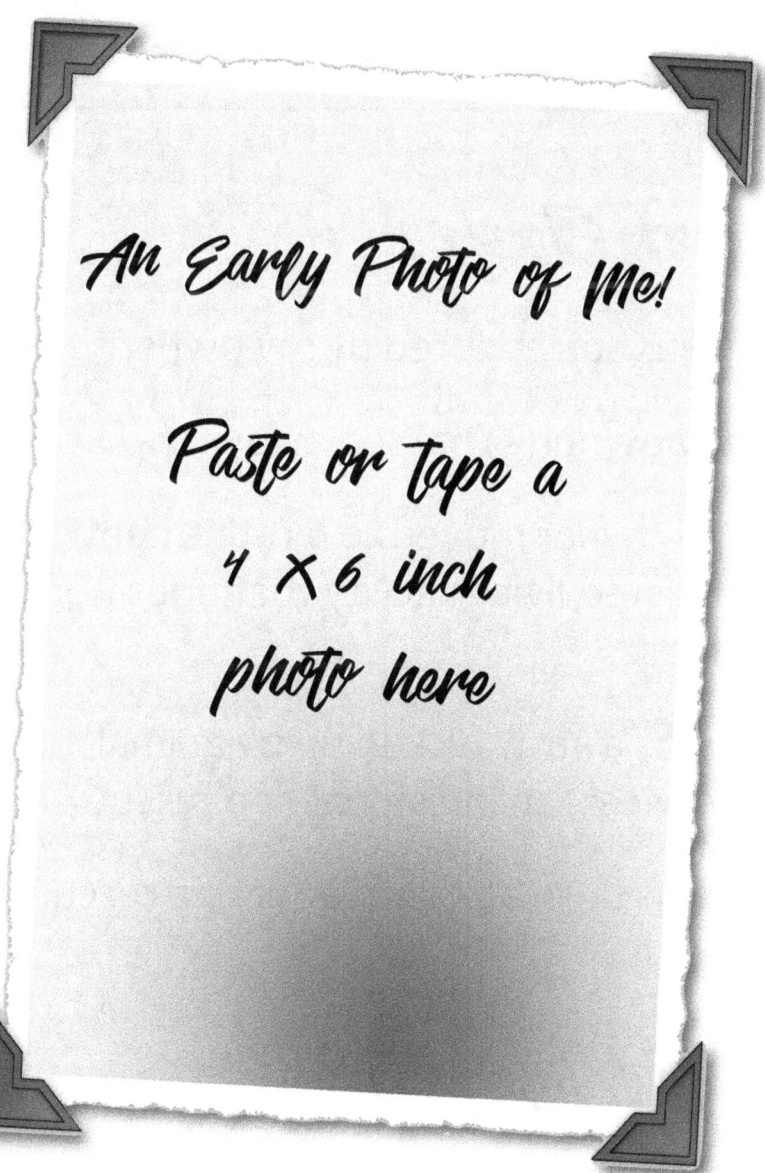

A Little About Me

My Original Name _____

My Given Name _____

My Date of Birth _____

My Breed _____

My Back Story

- ❑   I was surrendered by my owner.
- ❑   My owner(s) passed away.
- ❑   My owner moved to a retirement/assisted-living facility that does not allow dogs.
- ❑   I was a stray picked up by animal services, an individual or a rescue group.
- ❑   I was born at a shelter/with a rescue group.

Additional Information

_____

_____

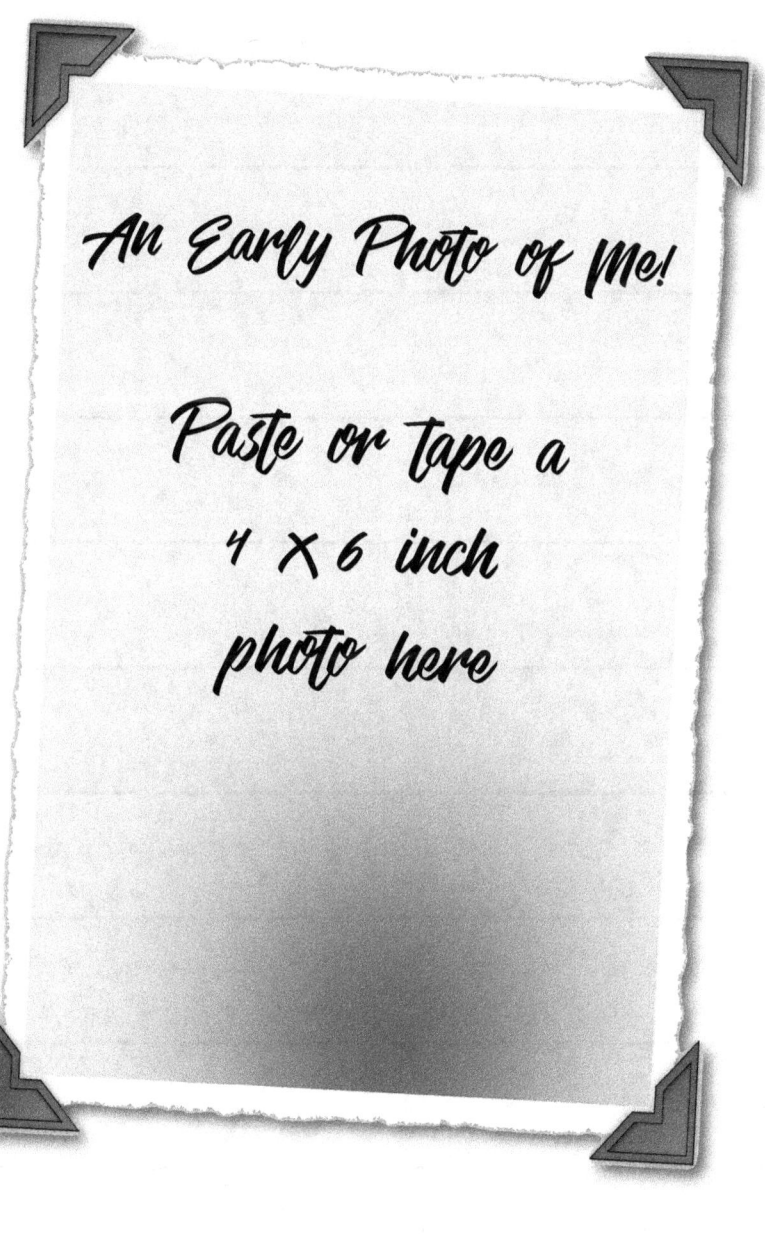

My "Back Story" in Detail

My Age on the Day I Went Home _____

Photo©pixabay.com/realworkhard

Important People in My Life

My Veterinarian _____

Clinic Name _____

Street Address _____

City _____ State _____ Zip _____

Phone Number _____

My Foster Mom and Dad _____

Street Address _____

City _____ State _____ Zip _____

Phone Number _____

E-Mail Address _____

My Vaccination History

Date	My Age	Vaccine

My Well-Being Treatments

Dates of Heartworm Preventative

_____   _____   _____   _____

_____   _____   _____   _____

_____   _____   _____   _____

_____   _____   _____   _____

_____   _____   _____   _____

Dates of Flea and Tick Preventative

_____   _____   _____   _____

_____   _____   _____   _____

_____   _____   _____   _____

_____   _____   _____   _____

My Veterinary Visits

Date _____

My Weight _____

Veterinarian _____

Diagnosis _____

Treatment _____

_____

Date _____

My Weight _____

Veterinarian _____

Diagnosis _____

Treatment _____

_____

Photo©123rf.com/Ian Allenden

My Veterinary Visits

Date _____

My Weight _____

Veterinarian _____

Diagnosis _____

Treatment _____

_____

Date _____

My Weight _____

Veterinarian _____

Diagnosis _____

Treatment _____

_____

My Dental Records

Date _____

Veterinarian _____

Tooth Extractions ❑ YES   ❑ NO

Follow-Up Treatment _____

_____

_____

Date _____

Veterinarian _____

Tooth Extractions ❑ YES   ❑ NO

Follow-Up Treatment _____

_____

_____

My Dental Records

Date _____

Veterinarian _____

Tooth Extractions ❏ YES   ❏ NO

Follow-Up Treatment _____
_____
_____

Date _____

Veterinarian _____

Tooth Extractions ❏ YES   ❏ NO

Follow-Up Treatment _____
_____
_____

My Favorite Foods

Brands of Kibble _____

_____

_____

What Time of Day Kibble is Given

☐ 1 _____ AM

☐ 2 _____ PM

Other Mealtime Foods I Enjoy

_____ _____

_____ _____

_____ _____

Photo©123rf.com/damedeeso

My Favorite Snacks and Treats

Brands of Treats   _____

                                  _____

                                  _____

What Time of Day Treats are Given

- ☐ 1 _____ AM   ☐ 1 _____ AM
- ☐ 2 _____ PM   ☐ 2 _____ PM

Fruits and Vegetables I Love to Nibble On

- ☐ Apple
- ☐ Banana
- ☐ Blueberries
- ☐ Raw Broccoli
- ☐ Cooked Broccoli
- ☐ Cantaloupe
- ☐ Raw Carrots
- ☐ Cooked Carrots
- ☐ Celery
- ☐ Cucumber
- ☐ Fresh Green Beans
- ☐ Cooked Green Beans
- ☐ Mango
- ☐ Oranges
- ☐ Peaches
- ☐ Pineapple
- ☐ Strawberries
- ☐ Watermelon
- ☐ _____ Other

My Special Dietary Needs

_____   _____

_____   _____

_____   _____

_____   _____

_____   _____

My Known Food Allergies

_____   _____

_____   _____

_____   _____

_____   _____

_____   _____

My Favorite Toys and Games

Photo©pixabay.com/Alexas_Fotos

_____

_____ _____

_____ _____

_____ _____

_____ _____

I like to play fetch with a ball or a stick	❏ YES	❏ NO
I like to play Tug of War with a rope toy	❏ YES	❏ NO
I like to retrieve a flying disc	❏ YES	❏ NO
I like to play Hide and Seek	❏ YES	❏ NO
Other games I like to play	_____	

My Favorite Outdoor Activities

Playing at the beach	☐ YES	☐ NO
Going to the park	☐ YES	☐ NO
Hiking	☐ YES	☐ NO
Boating	☐ YES	☐ NO
Taking a walk	☐ YES	☐ NO
Riding in a car	☐ YES	☐ NO
Swimming	☐ YES	☐ NO

Other Activities I Enjoy

_____

_____

_____

_____

My Sleeping Habits

I am the first one up in the morning	❏ YES	❏ NO
I sleep in until my human gets out of bed	❏ YES	❏ NO
I sleep with my human on the bed	❏ YES	❏ NO
I prefer to sleep in my own bed next to my human's bed	❏ YES	❏ NO
Before bed, I always have my favorite treat: _____	❏ YES	❏ NO

I cannot go to sleep without my favorite:
❏ Toy
❏ Blanket

Things You Need to Know About Me

I am afraid of lightning and/or thunder	☐ YES	☐ NO
I am afraid of fireworks and/or loud noises	☐ YES	☐ NO
I like to burrow in a blanket	☐ YES	☐ NO
I get along well with cats and kittens	☐ YES	☐ NO
I play well with small dogs	☐ YES	☐ NO
I play well with large dogs	☐ YES	☐ NO
I am a good watchdog	☐ YES	☐ NO
I am nervous around people I don't know	☐ YES	☐ NO
I like to snuggle on the couch with my human	☐ YES	☐ NO

My Training Experience

Puppy Classes ☐ YES ☐ NO

Instructor: _____

Basic Obedience ☐ YES ☐ NO

Instructor: _____

Advanced Obedience ☐ YES ☐ NO

Instructor: _____

Flyball ☐ YES ☐ NO

Instructor: _____

Agility ☐ YES ☐ NO

Instructor: _____

Other Class _____

Instructor: _____

Commands I Know

Sit	❑ YES	❑ NO
Stay	❑ YES	❑ NO
Down	❑ YES	❑ NO
Roll Over	❑ YES	❑ NO
Shake	❑ YES	❑ NO
High Five	❑ YES	❑ NO
Come	❑ YES	❑ NO

Other Commands

_____

_____

_____

_____

Photo©123rf.com/Susan-Richey-Schmitz

My Potty Habits

I am completely housebroken ☐ YES ☐ NO

I let my human know when I need a potty break ☐ YES ☐ NO

I have been trained to use puppy pads ☐ YES ☐ NO

My Typical Potty Times:

_____ AM

_____ AM

_____ AM

_____ AM

_____ PM

_____ PM

_____ PM

_____ PM

Additional Notes About Me

Also by Candace T. Botha

- I'm Going Home...Finally!—A Handbook of Everything You Need to Know About Your Newly Adopted Kitten or Cat - July 2017
- Forever in My Heart...A Journal for Families Who Lovingly Foster Cats & Kittens - January 2016
- Forever in My Heart...A Journal for Foster Pup Families - January 2016
- The Ultimate Editorial Planning Guide for Publishers & Editors - November 2015
- The Ultimate Assignment Journal for Freelance Photographers - October 2015
- The Ultimate Assignment Journal for Freelance Writers - September 2015
- How Blessed Am I?—A Weekly Journal for Giving Thanks for Life's Extraordinary Moments...Honoring the Watercolor Artistry of Carol M. Botha - March 2016

All journals are available online at www.Amazon.com, www.BarnesandNoble.com and other online book retailers

Suncoast Pet
Magazine

Published six times a year, Suncoast Pet is Southwest Florida's leading, award-winning pet publication, bringing community pet owners health and wellness articles written by local veterinarians and animal experts, profiles on people and businesses in the pet community, a spotlight on exciting new products for pets, a "Rescue Me" section of adoptable dogs and cats, contests, giveaways and so much more! Read the magazine from cover to cover online by visiting our website:

www.SuncoastPet.com

www.ingramcontent.com/pod-product-compliance
Lightning Source LLC
LaVergne TN
LVHW011901060526
838200LV00054B/4467